# The Book of 35 Peacock Stress Relieving Designs for Adults & Kids Relaxatio

# This Coloring Book Is Belongs To

___________________________________

___________________________________

___________________________________

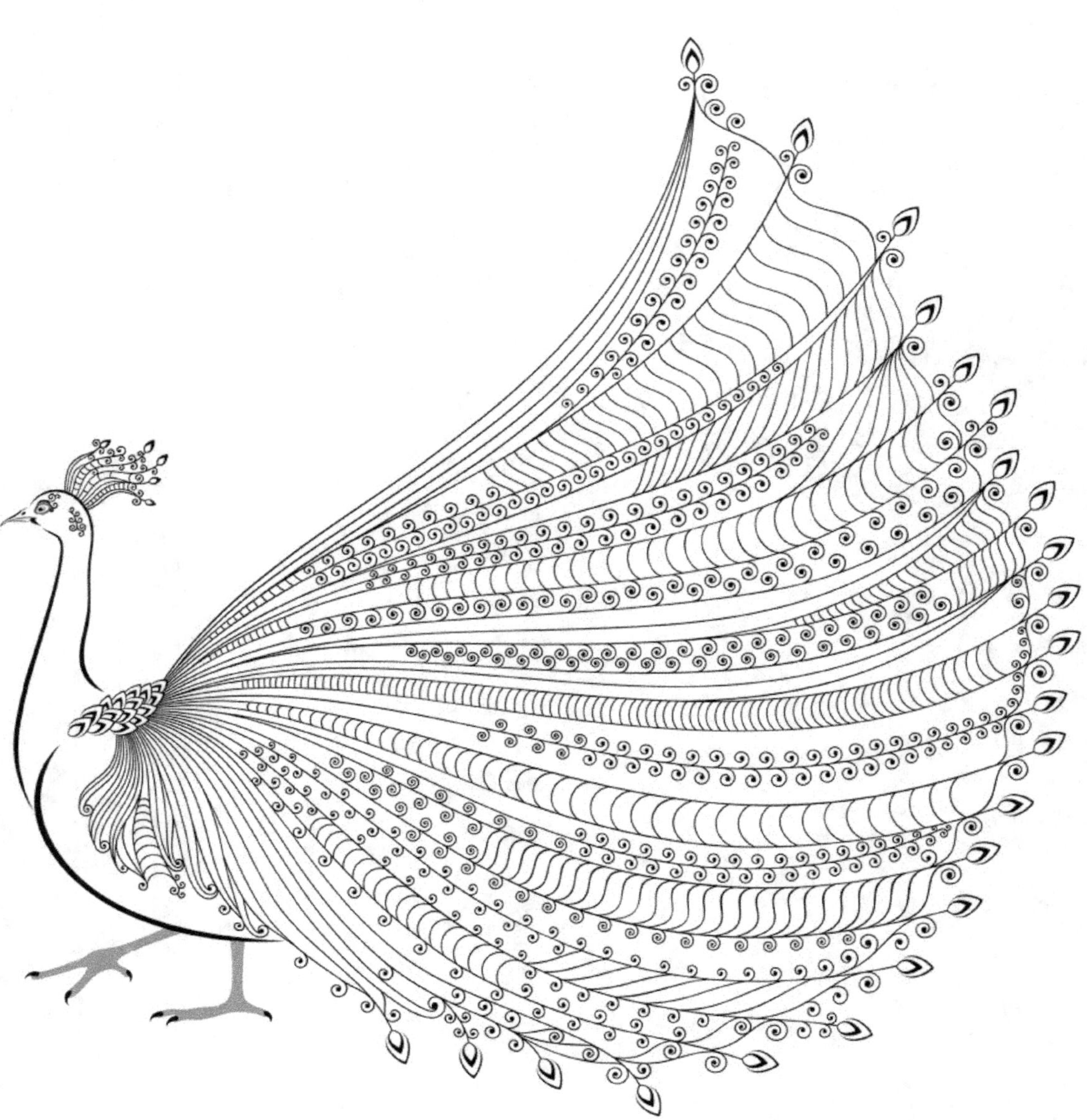

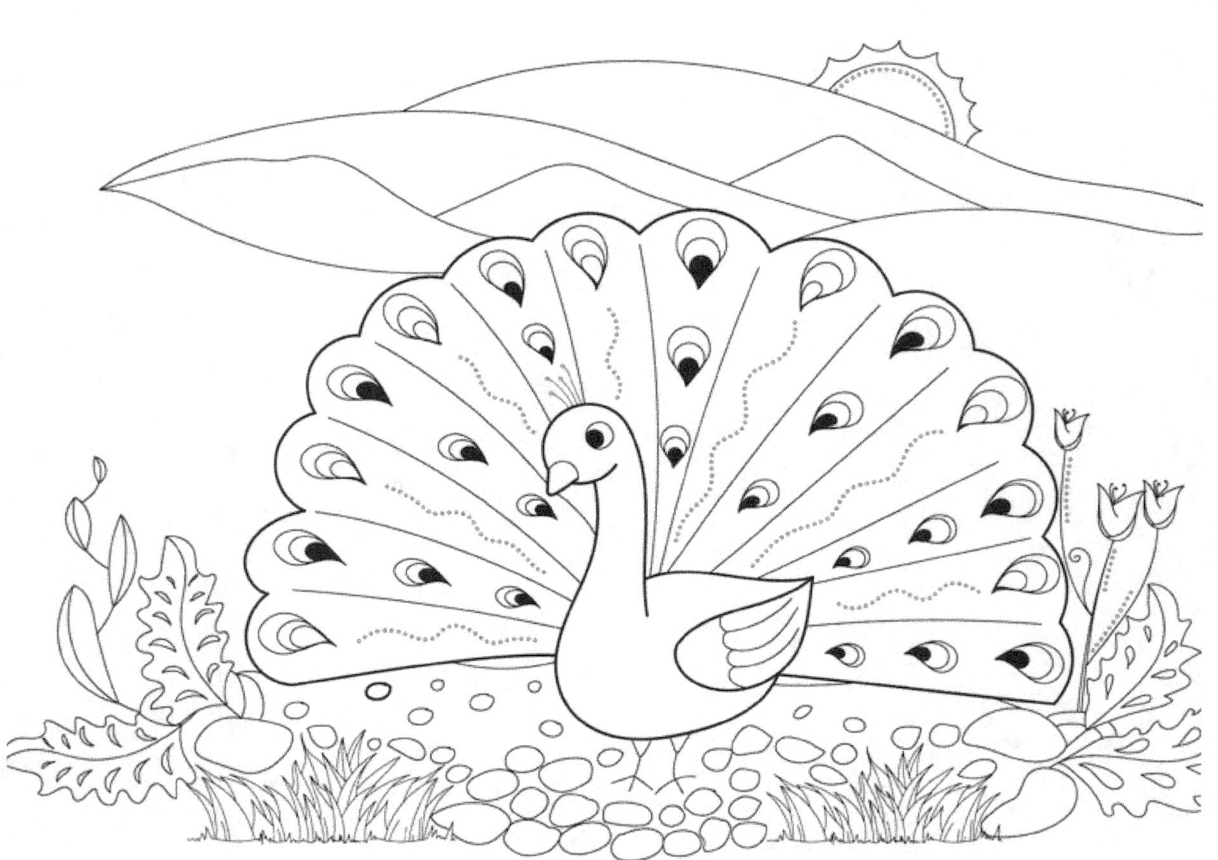

www.ingramcontent.com/pod-product-compliance
Lightning Source LLC
Chambersburg PA
CBHW081318250726
48662CB00008B/2642